HAROLD KLEMP

# TRUTH
# HAS NO
# SECRETS

## HAROLD KLEMP

ECKANKAR
Minneapolis

ABOUT THIS BOOK: *Truth Has No Secrets* is compiled from Harold Klemp's writings. These selections originally appeared in his books published by Eckankar.

**Truth Has No Secrets**
Copyright © 2005 ECKANKAR

Printed in USA.
Compiled by John Kulick
Edited by Joan Klemp, Anthony Moore,
and Mary Carroll Moore
Cover photo by Jim Brandenburg/Minden Pictures
Text photo by Robert Huntley
Cover design by Doug Munson

Library of Congress Cataloging-in-Publication Data
Klemp, Harold.
    Truth has no secrets / Harold Klemp.
        p. cm.
    ISBN 1-57043-218-X (hardcover : alk. paper)
    I. Spiritual life—Eckankar (Organization) I. Title.
BP605.E3K5748 2005
299'.93—dc22

                                    2005009836


∞ This paper meets the requirements of ANSI/NISO Z39.48-1992 (Permanence of Paper).

# CONTENTS

Dear Reader . . . . . . . . . . . . . . . . . . . . . . . . . vi

Love Comes First . . . . . . . . . . . . . . . . . . . . I

The Right of Choice . . . . . . . . . . . . . . . . . 13

A Larger Room . . . . . . . . . . . . . . . . . . . . . 25

Recognizing God's Help . . . . . . . . . . . . . . 37

A Broader View of Truth . . . . . . . . . . . . . . 49

The Next Step . . . . . . . . . . . . . . . . . . . . . . . 61

The Secret of Love . . . . . . . . . . . . . . . . . . . 73

Every Minute Counts . . . . . . . . . . . . . . . . . 85

Truth Has No Secrets . . . . . . . . . . . . . . . . . 97

A Life of Greater Happiness . . . . . . . . . . . 109

About the Author . . . . . . . . . . . . . . . . . . . . 121

# DEAR READER

*Truth Has No Secrets* is the third volume in Harold Klemp's award-winning Immortality of Soul Series.

The purpose of this book is to help us realize a broader view of truth. How? By seeing from Soul's higher viewpoint, which is centered in divine love.

In *Truth Has No Secrets*, Harold Klemp encourages us to look at life and our experiences from Soul's spiritual perspective. Harold Klemp says Soul does not think, It perceives. To perceive means to become aware of something as it really is. Herein lies the key to unraveling the mysteries of today so they are no longer mysteries tomorrow.

Take one quote each day, and contemplate its meaning. Ask Divine Spirit to show you how to unlock its wisdom from Soul's viewpoint. The keys to living a life of greater love, purpose, and happiness are at your fingertips.

# $\mathcal{L}$OVE COMES FIRST

---

$\mathcal{L}$ove God first, and then love your neighbor as yourself.

$\mathcal{L}$ove your neighbor as yourself doesn't mean a lot more than yourself. It means you have to love yourself before you can love your neighbor.

Love yourself. That means you have to have a good opinion of yourself as a spiritual being.

*Y*ou are a child of God. Why not have a good healthy opinion about yourself? You are worth something.

If you can carry this with you, then you can go out into the world and love your neighbor as yourself. Then, but not before. If you can do this truly from your heart, this will be an entirely different world.

*L*ife is a series of experiences all put together: the big, the little, the important, the unimportant. So we go through this journey of Soul, becoming more god-like in wisdom and in divine love as we move forward spiritually.

*T*he purpose of divine love is to encourage the independence and ability of another to survive and thrive spiritually. How? It is by way of God's Light and Sound, the two elements that are the Holy Spirit, the Voice of God, the Creative Force in all the universes, the ECK.

*S*oul's whole purpose for being in this world is to find divine love.

Begin with the love you have. Love gratefully. This love expands your heart into a greater vessel which can hold yet more love. On the outside, divine and emotional love may look the same, but divine love is joyful, thankful. It gives itself fully.

You ask, "What is my mission in life?" Very specifically, it is to become a Co-worker with God. How this breaks down for your particular talents is actually between God and you. It's not for me to say.

If you love your work, your profession, or whatever you're doing, then you'll have some idea what it means to be a Co-worker with God. It simply means that you're doing what you want to do, what you enjoy doing.

*T*he spiritual life is carrying out the duties that we have accepted, such as family and children, and figuring out ways to support them. This is where the challenge of life is today.

You find that love comes in small ways and small places. And those ways and places are just as precious as when love comes in a big wave.

To get love we must give love, and the same is true, spiritually, of freedom. To have freedom we must give freedom—and you find that the more you are able to give, the more you get.

*P*ractice the love. Practice God is Love. Practice tolerance and compassion.

When love is on the field, fear must retreat.

# THE RIGHT OF CHOICE

*T*he right of choice: It's our attitude—the way we look at things—that often determines whether we are happy or miserable, whether we are full of love or full of fear.

*I*n ECK we realize we are in the right place at the right time, no matter what our circumstances may be.

*T*hanksgiving is one of the attributes or qualities that come to the person who loves God. To serve others is to love others, and to love others is to serve others.

*R*ecognize that something greater than walking any particular path is to be able to exercise the freedom to choose for yourself the path to God that is right for you, and furthermore, to allow the same freedom for others.

*We* don't make a goal of higher ethics, but higher ethics are a natural result of increased spiritual unfoldment. This ought to show in our lives, in our business dealings, and in our interactions with others.

*Y*ou learn that you are totally responsible for everything that you do. That everything that comes into your life has come back to you.

This is a hard lesson for people because it totally wipes out the victim consciousness.

When we move into new areas of consciousness, we find that our whole life must change around us. We have to live by new rules.

*Y*ou make a conscious effort to align yourself or put yourself in tune with Divine Spirit. And you do that by chanting a spiritual word, such as HU (pronounced like the word *hue*). HU is an ancient name for God. It is also a love song to God. You sing it silently or aloud, with love in your heart.

*D*ivine Spirit is not a person. "A force" is not even the correct way to speak of It. The best we can usually do is to say It's the Light and Sound of God, the Voice of God, the creative force that made all creation.

*A*s Soul, you have the God-knowledge within you. My main job is to awaken the knowledge and love for the divine things that are already in your heart. You are Soul. You are a child of God.

And your spiritual destiny is to become a Co-worker with God, to spread divine love to all those around you.

*You* do what gives you the chance for the most spiritual growth and personal fulfillment. That is what it is like to be a Co-worker with God.

# A LARGER ROOM

*E*ach morning you should be awaking in a larger room, in a larger state of spiritual consciousness where you say, "Well, I wonder what life has to teach me today."

*T*ake responsibility. Recognize that this entire lifetime is a high spiritual experience—or it could be. Whether or not it will be depends upon how you look at it. It depends upon your attitude.

*T*ake the lessons of life as teachers and not as crutches. If you can just remember this—the concept of a larger room—it will help you immensely.

*A*s we go into middle age, we enter a larger room with new experiences. As we go from middle age to advanced age, we find we go to still another room. And each room should always be larger—where we have new experiences. We have to deal with things that used to be easy and suddenly we find they're not.

The whole thing about Soul is survival. Taking care of our health is certainly one of the strongest aspects of survival here.

As Soul goes farther on the path to God, It develops the gift of randomity, which means being able to move here, there, or anywhere. To other people, it looks like a random walk. But to the individual under the guidance of Divine Spirit, it's walking the path of Light and Sound, the Light and Sound of God.

*T*ake responsibility for yourself, for your condition in life. No matter how bad a situation is, even at work.

*You've* just entered a larger room, and that's often why you feel this emptiness. It takes a little while for divine love to reach in and touch all the corners of your heart.

*Gratitude is the secret of love.*

*As* a spiritual exercise, take yourself into a larger room. For example, if you have a desire for self-discipline, leave the room of self-discipline that you're in. Go down the corridor, and go into another room. This room will be larger. It will be much larger. Just live within the awareness that you want to be in this room of more self-discipline. Then let the Holy Spirit, the ECK, bring about the changes in your life that will accompany such a resolution.

*Y*ou will find as you move forward on the path to God and unfold spiritually that you will become more filled with divine love, and you will have more kindness and compassion for other people. In so doing, you will eventually become a Co-worker with God.

# RECOGNIZING GOD'S HELP

*W*e don't learn and grow if everything is always smooth and pretty and nice. Sometimes you have to get the other experiences in life. It's necessary, like salt and pepper on your food. It adds spice to life.

We're talking about recognizing God's help in your life. This help is like little presents. But oftentimes we don't think of them as presents.

The reason life gives us more lessons is because we can handle more. We've learned the old lessons, the ABCs. Now we can go on to arithmetic and geography and other things.

*I*nstead of talking about all we know, at times it pays to just listen. Listen to the people around you. If someone's telling you something spiritual and positive, this is from the Voice of God.

Things that are negative and destructive to you are from the negative side. Do not do them—no matter how spiritual the person is who says to.

*S*oul's lesson here is to learn how to love God through loving first ourselves and then our family.

*I*f you're going to do anything, do it for love or don't do it at all.

*I*f fear and guilt is a part of your upbringing, it can also cause a lot of problems for you in such things as work and health.

If you can learn to forgive yourself first—and to accept forgiveness—then maybe you can forgive others. Then you can find this healing, because the love of God comes through the Holy Spirit. It is the Holy Spirit.

*D*ivine Spirit has Its own hand in our affairs to save us from trouble of a more serious kind.

*S*ometimes the Holy Spirit works in whatever way It can. It knows our soft spots.

The Holy Spirit gives us lessons. If we have the capacity for love—which is all that this life is about—life gives us more experience.

*I*t's very popular on television to talk about the Light, but people don't know about the other aspect, the Sound. In Its fullest sense, this Voice of God is the Holy Spirit. God speaks to us with Its voice—the Holy Spirit—in one way or another.

Often we don't recognize God's help—which usually means God's love. We don't recognize it, but other people see it in us.

We're told in some of our human scriptures that God's love is basically an indefinable thing. It's a feeling, more or less. But in ECK we say that you can see it and you can hear it.

And when this divine love comes into you, it will change you. It changes your state of consciousness. Degree by degree, it makes you a new person.

# A BROADER VIEW OF TRUTH

*T*he spiritual path is not about power. It's about love.

*T*hose of you who have moved through several different levels of spiritual consciousness have found that your life can get rough at times. Why? Not because somebody in the dark alley is shooting arrows at you. It's because you're meeting yourself. And this *is* truth.

Truth means meeting yourself.

One of the first things you learn on the path of ECK is that there is no separation between the physical life—your everyday life—and your spiritual life. Carrying this a step further, there is no separation between you and the dream world. These are all part of you.

*C*hildren have the wisdom of God and are closer to it than many people who have spent years in this world gaining all kinds of knowledge about the nature of religion. Children have it naturally.

*I*n the future, some clever scientist will come up with some way to prove that animals and people are more than just the mind. There's something beyond the mind. The animating feature in a living being is not the mind but Soul.

And what is Soul? It is you, the real being.

*S*ome people don't believe in a state of consciousness for animals. These are the people who feel that God's love is limited to human beings. If these same people were living in the Middle Ages, they would be the ones who'd say, "God's love is limited to earth. Therefore, earth is the center of the universe."

Always remember you're not alone. Spirit is always with us, always guiding, always protecting, always attempting to bring joy and make our life better, but that doesn't mean that we are always aware and listening.

The greater states of consciousness mean more freedom to live, move, and do as we wish.

We serve God and life out of gratitude. Why? For the blessings we have received.

What is the greatest blessing? The gift of life itself. It's living. It's getting more experience in life, learning more about who and what you are.

The more you learn about yourself, the more you have to give back to life. It's natural. You have to. Your heart opens, you have greater capacity for love. To get more love, you have to give more love. As you give more, you get more.

Whether or not your philosophy or religion accepts Souls in forms other than the human is unimportant. If you can accept reincarnation and the fact that Soul takes on many different bodies, you will find much more joy and happiness in your own life. You'll also find greater understanding of God's creation.

*A*s sure as you're alive, if you can make it over the next hurdle, through the next stormy sea, your view of life will change. So will your viewpoint on truth. Why? Because the experience made you wiser. You will have a broader view of truth.

# THE
# NEXT STEP

*E*arth is a schoolroom for Soul. Soul must learn all the spiritual lessons of life before It can gain spiritual freedom.

At some point, people will get a little further along the spiritual path and understand that the responsibility for their spiritual unfoldment begins and ends with themselves.

*I*t begins at home, with yourself. Before we can help anybody else, we must first be able to help ourselves.

When life dishes it out to us, try to take it in stride.

*A* waking dream is something that happens in the outer, everyday life that has spiritual significance.

*Divine* Spirit helps those who are ready to drop some habit that's standing in their way on the spiritual path to God.

*S*oul Travel just means getting in touch with your higher nature, which is Soul. Soul Travel means moving from the human state of consciousness to the Soul state of consciousness.

*L*earning spiritual consciousness is learning how to live in this world no matter what comes. We learn through spiritual exercises how to live life graciously, from childhood to old age.

We learn how to live life in the best way possible.

These spiritual exercises link you with the guidance of the Holy Spirit, which is seen as Light and heard as Sound.

It is important for an individual who hopes to make any advancement on the spiritual path to have these two aspects, the twin pillars of God, in his life.

*T*hese experiences give you a vitality and insight into life that you haven't had before.

$\mathcal{O}$ften when you first come to a true spiritual path, you find your karma speeds up. You are more alive than you've ever been before. But sometimes you wish you weren't because you're scrambling—you're using every bit of your spiritual creativity to figure out what to do next.

Just remember to sing HU as a spiritual exercise and ask, "What do I do now?" Then wait and watch for the Holy Spirit to open a way for you to go to the next step in your spiritual life.

# THE SECRET OF LOVE

*B*eyond experience is something much more important, and this is simply learning how to give and receive God's love. That's not experience. That's a condition. That's being able to open your heart, to open your wings, to accept the gifts of life.

The gifts are all around you all the time. Most often they come to us as acts of kindness by people near us.

*D*ivine Spirit will touch you in some way, in some unexpected way. It will lift you spiritually.

*H*U is the love song to God that we sing. It's to open your heart—like opening your wings. Opening your wings simply means opening your state of consciousness.

*L*ove those who are close to you with your whole heart, but love those who are outside of your close circle with a detached love, with charity.

In other words, you cannot love everyone with the same warmth. Loving means acting and showing your love. The human body can give only so much love and usually we reserve the warm love for those who are close to us. And they do the same for us, their loved one.

*L*ove does everything for those it loves.

*I*t's the nature of an open consciousness to simply love and give of God's love
to other people. But even more important
is to receive it. To receive the blessings that
are all around us.

*S*oul is immortal. It has no begin-ning nor ending.

*S*ometimes Divine Spirit will give you an insight into something that's happening in your daily life. One of the most interesting ways is through an experience of a past life.

*If* you believe Soul is born within the realm of time and space, you can't really say It's without a beginning. It has a beginning in time and space, if you're going to look at it that way. But God created Soul before the worlds began.

Soul merely comes here as part of Its experience from the other worlds beyond time and space. It comes here and has many, many lifetimes learning one thing or another.

The greatest thing Soul learns is how to love God. Our experiences teach us how to love God.

The water of life, even as truth, appears to be available everywhere to everyone. But only those who know how to give love are able to drink of it, to receive truth.

# EVERY MINUTE COUNTS

---

*O*ur goal in this life is not to find out how to use Spirit in our life, but how to open ourselves as a vehicle for Divine Spirit to use as It will. Life becomes an adventure. We are opened to learning in a way we have never been before.

*I*f we give up to Spirit as It leads us into a greater awareness, we can build and expand into a greater life. It's when we hold back—when Spirit opens the door and we refuse to walk through—that we find life becomes difficult.

*T*he greatest thing we learn on the path of ECK is to live in the moment. Once we've done the best we can, we put the rest into the hands of God.

There is a saying that there are really no secret teachings, that everything we need to know is available to us on an open shelf somewhere. But it depends upon our state of consciousness to accept it.

On the spiritual path we are looking for self-responsibility. If we have created a debt, we're going to have to pay it back. It's the spiritual law.

This debt is called karma. We pay off only as much as is necessary to gain an understanding of the spiritual law which we have repeatedly broken, whether in this lifetime or a previous one.

The spiritual path can be an easy one. It means giving up our preformed ideas of what spirituality is and what it is not.

*D*o the best you can. Be the best you can. That's the bottom line. Because in trying to do and be the best, you are trying to express a quality of God, the divine nature. You're trying to be the highest it's possible to be.

*S*ome people don't understand why they are here on earth. They wonder, *Is it to just put in my time until the final hour?* So you ask, Why waste my time living a very upright ethical life? Why bother?

Here's the reason to bother: It is that every minute counts. Every minute is an opportunity to develop the qualities of divine love and mercy.

*Y*ou start with the people who are closest to you. You show them warm love. To people in general, you give another kind of love, what the Bible calls charity. This is detached love.

In other words, you have goodwill toward all people, but toward your loved ones—the ones who are close to you in your family—you give warm love.

*L*ife is something to live joyfully. Live it joyfully because you're learning to be a Co-worker with God.

This means practice the God qualities even on the days you don't feel like practicing the God qualities. These are the times it's really hard to practice your spiritual disciplines.

*S*ometimes truth is bitter. Sometimes it's harsh. And sometimes for this reason we aren't able to recognize it. Because when we look at truth, we look at it through our state of consciousness—through our eyes, through our experience—not just from this lifetime but from every past lifetime. The more experience we have, the more we are able to discern truth.

# TRUTH HAS NO SECRETS

*Y*ou develop a sense of humor, and as challenges come up, you begin to draw on your creativity. You find solutions that would never have occurred to you before.

Life becomes more fun—you actually have a more adventuresome life. You get put into situations you would not have been in before, because you are going one step beyond yourself. And as you get yourself in trouble, you also have help to get out of it, because as you learn to work with your own resources, you are developing self-mastery.

The spiritual truths are secret only until the state of consciousness becomes unlocked. Divine Spirit is able to unlock the consciousness a little at a time so that we can get the deeper understandings.

We are learning to work with intuition, which actually is Soul giving us gentle guidance to make our life better.

*S*oul doesn't think, It perceives.

*W*orking with the creative power of Soul means learning how to focus your attention. It's something you have to work with, because if you're going to be good in anything, you have to put some effort into it.

*A* principle of Soul is to be timely. If you're going to set a framework in this world, if you're going to set a goal, also set a deadline to accomplish it. What are you going to do and when will you finish it?

No matter what it is, set yourself a goal and a deadline, because this is how you begin working with the creative imagination.

As you go further on the spiritual path, it may become harder but it also becomes more honest. You now know exactly what you're doing. You become willing to accept total responsibility for your actions. You watch your actions much more carefully.

*I*n the spiritual works it says something to the effect that unless you become as little children, you cannot enter into the kingdom of heaven. It means this fresh consciousness that looks at life through eyes that have never seen before. Everything is new to a child. They have no preconceived notions of how something should be.

*A*s you gain in spiritual unfoldment, everyone in your circle of acquaintances is benefited and uplifted.

*M*ost people don't understand the nature of truth. We think truth is always kind and gentle. That is erroneous.

Truth means not just hearing something someone says to you and saying, "Oh, that is truth, that is wisdom." It's living it. If people know truth, they will live it. That means showing consideration for their family and friends, showing love and respect even when they're not feeling like it. Even saying thank you when we don't feel like saying thank you.

*T*ruth is never hidden. It's always available for the Soul who wants to take the next step.

# $\mathscr{A}$ LIFE OF GREATER HAPPINESS

*S*piritual liberation is what we are looking for. It actually comes at a point we call Self-Realization, which means that we have been freed from the cares of this world. I'm not saying we no longer have problems, but we now have an understanding of those things which come into our life that must be faced.

We see where they came from, how we caused them, and what to do about them so we can live a life of greater happiness.

*O*ne of the spiritual principles I have learned is there is always a way, no matter what. If we have a health, financial, or some other kind of situation—there is always a way out.

We are able to figure our way out.

*A*s the Light and Sound of God come in, we experience a spiritual upliftment that takes us above materialism.

This doesn't mean we now give up our material possessions, but it does mean giving up our undue attachment to these material things. We do not stop loving our family and friends, but we do give up undue attachment to them.

We have experiences with Divine Spirit and begin developing an understanding of what is happening in our daily life. We also develop a sense of humor and tolerance when things don't go the way we've planned.

*S*pirit will use you no matter where you are. You may or may not be conscious of this Light and Sound of God coming in, but you find a way to give It back to other people.

You simply give back some service of love to the world, to your friend, your neighbor; and it may be simply by doing a good deed every day no one ever knows about.

*T*his Light and Sound is important for Soul. It is direct communication with God. This is how God communicates—through the ECK, Divine Spirit, also known as the Holy Ghost, Comforter, Nam, or whatever you want to call It.

*Y*ou and I are Soul. Each of us is a unique creation, a spark of God. There are no two of us alike. Those of us who have similar ideas about life, gained from our personal experiences, may get together in a group and call it a church or a fellowship.

We are on the path to God in our own way, at our own time, and each of us ought to have this freedom to find God as we will.

When you come to the state of self-mastery, it does not mean you now have poetic license to live life doing whatever you please.

It simply means that now you know and understand the laws of Spirit as they apply to you. You know the things you can do and the things you cannot do. And while you make your way through life with these guidelines, you also are being a vehicle for Spirit.

*A* debt to God that has been created must be repaid by the one who incurred the debt. This is the Law of Life: Whatsoever a man sows, that also shall he reap.

*O*f course, there is an even greater law, and this is the Law of Love. This is the Law of Spirit, the Light and Sound of God.

You can bring It into your own life, and when you do, there will be no one who can take It from you or tell you this or that way is right for you. You are going to know for yourself from direct experience with the Light and Sound of God.

*O*ften we look for the key to the spiritual worlds and wonder where it is. Many times it's so close—right in front of us—actually within us.

There's an old story that when God made this world, man, and all creation, He said, "But Soul is a precious thing, and I want to put It somewhere safe. I believe I'll just put It in the heart of man; he'll never think to look for It there."

## About the Author

Author Harold Klemp is known as a pioneer of today's focus on "everyday spirituality." He was raised on a Wisconsin farm and attended divinity school.

In 1981, after years of training, he became the spiritual leader of Eckankar, Religion of the Light and Sound of God. His mission is to help people find their way back to God in this life.

Harold Klemp speaks each year to thousands of seekers at Eckankar seminars. Author of more than forty-five books, he continues to write, including many articles and spiritual-study discourses. Harold Klemp's inspiring and practical approach to spirituality helps thousands of people worldwide find greater freedom, wisdom, and love in their lives.

ALSO BY
HAROLD KLEMP

Available at bookstores, online booksellers,
or directly from:
Eckankar
PO Box 2000  Chanhassen, MN 55317-2000 USA.
Tel (952) 380-2222  Fax (952) 380-2295
www.eckankar.org

*Immortality of Soul Series*
The Language of Soul
Love—The Keystone of Life
Truth Has No Secrets

*A selected list:*
Autobiography of a Modern Prophet
A Modern Prophet Answers Your Key Questions about Life